M000105980

Library Media Center
Israel Loring Elementary School
Sudbury, Ma

RECYCLING

ANGELA ROYSTON

**RAINTREE
STECK-VAUGHN**
PUBLISHERS
A Steck-Vaughn Company

Austin, Texas

ENVIRONMENT STARTS HERE!

TITLES IN THE SERIES
Food · Recycling · Transportation · Water

© Copyright 1999, text, Steck-Vaughn Company

All rights reserved. No part of this book may be reproduced or
utilized in any form or by any means, electronic or mechanical,
including photocopying, recording, or by any information storage
and retrieval system, without permission in writing from the
Publisher. Inquiries should be addressed to: Copyright Permissions,
Steck-Vaughn Company, P.O. Box 26015, Austin, TX 78755.

Published by Raintree Steck-Vaughn Publishers,
an imprint of Steck-Vaughn Company

Library of Congress Cataloging-in-Publication Data
Royston. Angela.
Recycling / Angela Royston.
      p.   cm.—(Environment starts here)
      Includes bibliographical references and index.
      Summary: Describes different kinds of waste and explains
      how recycling can be used to control waste and create less of it.
      ISBN 0-8172-5353-X
      1. Recycling (Waste, etc.)—Juvenile literature.
      [1. Recycling (Waste). 2. Refuse and refuse disposal.]
      I. Title. II. Series.
      TD794.5.R69 1999
      363.72'82—dc21   98-17741

Printed in Italy. Bound in the United States.
1 2 3 4 5 6 7 8 9 0 03 02 01 00 99

Picture Acknowledgments
Pages 1: Ecoscene/Nick Hawkes. 4: Eye Ubiquitous/Craig Hutchins. 7: Wayland Picture
Library. 9. Ecoscene/Lorenzo Lees. 10: Ecoscene/Ian Harwood. 11: Britstock/IFA-Bernard
Ducke. 12: Eye Ubiquitous/Steve Miller. 14: Zefa/Stockmarket. 15: Ecoscene/Kevin King.
16: Zefa/Stockmarket. 17: Britstock/IFA-Hans Jurgen Wiedl. 18: Eye Ubiquitous/Jim Winkley.
19: Ecoscene/Towse. 20: Ecoscene/Sally Morgan. 21: Eye Ubiquitous/Paul Seheult. 21(inset):
Ecoscene/Sally Morgan. 22: Wayland/Angus Blackburn. 23, 24, 25, 26: Zefa/Stockmarket.
27: Ecoscene/Rob Nichol. 28: Ecoscene/Stuart Donachie. 29: Zefa/Stockmarket.
Cover: Zefa/Stockmarket.
Illustrated by Rudi Vizi

The photo on page 1 shows children putting newspapers into a paper recycling container.

CONTENTS

TRASH AND WASTE   4
Packaging Material   6
Needless Waste   8
Bury It or Burn It?   10

WHAT IS RECYCLING?   13
Why Recycle?   14
Saving Energy   17
Sorting and Separating   18

NEW FROM OLD   20
Bottles and Cans   22
Recycling Plastic   25

REUSE   26

CREATING LESS WASTE   28

Glossary   30
Further Reading   31
Index   32

TRASH AND WASTE

Everyone throws out trash. You and your family probably fill several bags a week with waste paper, empty cans, plastic bottles and glass jars, food scraps, and other garbage.

In a street, empty cardboard and wooden boxes have been piled high, ready to be taken away by garbage collectors.

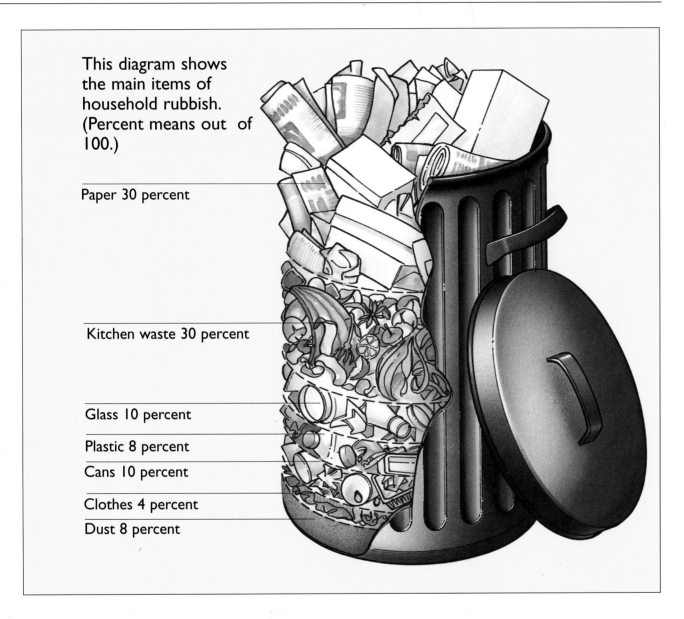

This diagram shows the main items of household rubbish. (Percent means out of 100.)

Paper 30 percent

Kitchen waste 30 percent

Glass 10 percent

Plastic 8 percent

Cans 10 percent

Clothes 4 percent

Dust 8 percent

Your school probably has several containers that fill up with paper, broken toys, and old pens. Over a year most families throw away between one and two tons of trash. That's how much an elephant weighs!

Packaging Material

Most of the trash in your garbage can is packaging from food and other goods. Food from the supermarket is often packaged in a can, plastic bag, or cardboard box, or is wrapped in cellophane.

The contents of a shopping bag shows a huge variety of packaging materials.

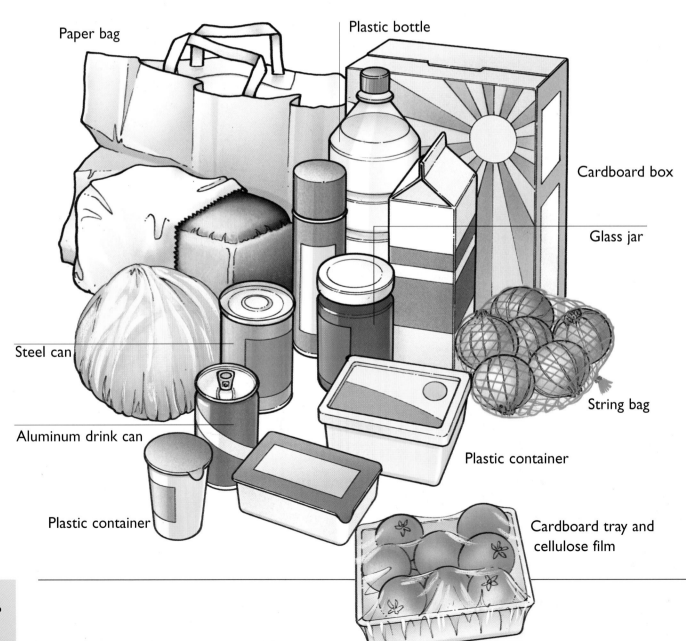

Paper bag

Plastic bottle

Cardboard box

Glass jar

Steel can

String bag

Aluminum drink can

Plastic container

Plastic container

Cardboard tray and cellulose film

Packaging keeps the food clean and protects it from being damaged. Packaging makes things look attractive and exciting, and it may give information, like instructions.

A boy and girl empty and sort through the contents of a trash can. Most of the waste is food-packaging material.

Needless Waste

Sometimes too much packaging is used. Computer games and toys often come in large boxes, with cardboard sections and advertising leaflets inside. This can make you think you are getting more for your money.

A girl unpacks the shopping and throws away unwanted packaging.

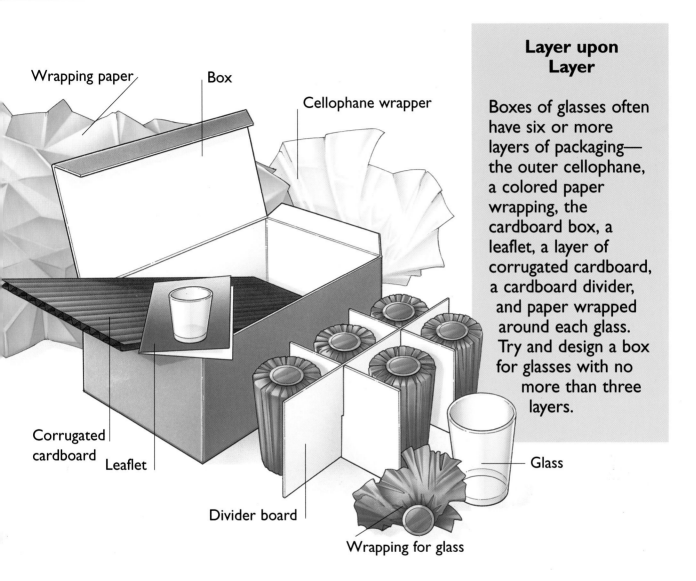

Wrapping paper   Box   Cellophane wrapper

Corrugated cardboard   Leaflet

Divider board

Wrapping for glass

Glass

Layer upon Layer

Boxes of glasses often have six or more layers of packaging—the outer cellophane, a colored paper wrapping, the cardboard box, a leaflet, a layer of corrugated cardboard, a cardboard divider, and paper wrapped around each glass. Try and design a box for glasses with no more than three layers.

Most stores and supermarkets give every customer a plastic shopping bag to take their shopping home, whether they need it or not. Although plastic bags and boxes can be used again, most people get new ones each time.

Bury It or Burn It?

We produce so much garbage that getting rid of it brings problems. Some garbage is burned in huge incinerators. Smoke from incinerators pollutes, or dirties, the air.

Some garbage is squashed flat and dumped into huge holes in the ground called landfill sites. As the garbage rots, it produces poisons. These can sometimes pollute nearby rivers and streams.

A bulldozer is used to flatten a pile of household garbage dumped on a landfill site.

Garbage trucks drive into an incineration plant to deliver their loads for burning.

Private
Fahrzeuge

Städtische
Fahrzeuge

11

A mechanical grab is used to sort through a pile of scrap metal from cars, refrigerators, and household machines.

WHAT IS RECYCLING?

Much garbage can be recycled instead of being thrown away. Recycling means using materials again to make something new. First, materials have to be sorted and separated into groups.

Empty glass jars can be washed and crushed. The glass can be recycled to make bottles. Paper, metal cans, plastics, and car oil can all be recycled, sometimes many times.

Household items that can be recycled. The shoes and clothes could be recycled or used by another person.

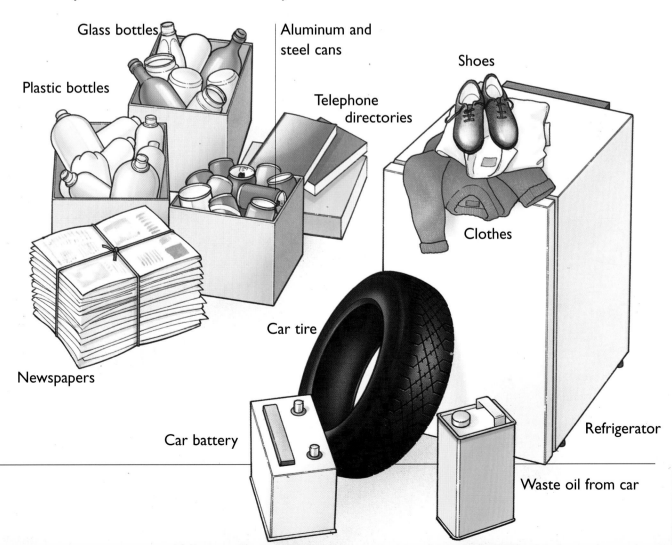

Glass bottles

Plastic bottles

Aluminum and steel cans

Telephone directories

Shoes

Clothes

Newspapers

Car tire

Car battery

Refrigerator

Waste oil from car

Why Recycle?

When you put aside everything that can be recycled, there is less garbage left to be buried or burned. This means less pollution from landfill sites and incinerators.

Recycling uses less of the earth's supply of resources or useful materials. For example, fewer trees are cut down when paper is recycled. This is because paper is usually made from trees.

Computers are made with expensive and rare metals and other materials that can be recycled. The plastic casing can also be reused.

Kitchen waste is piled on top of dead leaves to make compost. Compost is rotting vegetable matter that is recycled to fertilize growing plants.

Trees are cut from a forest to make wood pulp for paper. The huge logs have to be carried by truck to the paper mill.

Saving Energy

Making something from recycled materials uses less energy than making it from new materials. Most energy comes from coal, oil, or gas, and these are running out.

Recycling saves work as well as energy. Digging metals out of the ground and cutting down trees is not only difficult. It also uses gasoline for machines and electricity.

Sheets of steel being made from hot, molten iron. Coal must be burned to melt the iron. It is much easier and cheaper to make recycled steel.

Sorting and Separating

Materials that are going to be recycled must be sorted into different groups, such as paper, metal, glass, and plastic. The sorting starts when you put each type of material into a different bag.

These recycling bins are lined up outside a supermarket. The bins are marked for different types of materials.

Recycling Containers

Find out how recycling is organized in your area. Are there special cans at the supermarket for bottles or paper? Do you have to do anything to bottles or cans before you send them to be recycled?

Household trash is sorted by hand at a recycling center.

Bags of recyclable items may be picked up from your home by collectors, or you may have to take them to a recycling center.

At a recycling center, cardboard, paper, steel, and aluminum cans are separated. Glass is sorted into clear and other colors.

NEW FROM OLD

New paper is made by chopping and mashing wood into tiny pieces and then mixing it to a pulp with water. Old paper that is recycled simply has to be mixed with water to make new pulp.

All kinds of paper, even good-quality writing paper, can be made from recycled pulp. Look for the "recycled" sign on kitchen paper towels, toilet paper, and on cardboard and paper packaging.

At a recycling center in Jakarta, Indonesia, unwanted metal containers and boxes are broken up into flat sheets.

Waste paper is collected, mashed into a pulp, and then rolled into flat sheets. Recycled paper can be used for writing, drawing, or printing the pages of books.

Bottles and Cans

Some companies sell drinks in returnable glass bottles, which are collected, washed, and then used again. Reusing glass bottles uses less energy than crushing and melting old bottles to make new glass.

Children sort empty glass bottles by color and then load them into recycling containers.

In Malawi, watering cans made from recycled scrap metal are put on display for sale to local people.

Magnetic Sorter

Use a magnet to test whether a can is made of steel or aluminum. The magnet will stick to a steel can, but not to an aluminum one. Aluminum is more valuable than steel, so make sure you recycle it.

Steel can

Aluminum can   Aluminum foil

Most cans are made of steel, which can be recycled again and again. An empty can of beans could end up as a spoon, as part of a car, or as paper clips!

The fleecy jacket and hat worn by this mountaineer are filled with fibers made from recycled plastic. The fibers trap body heat, keeping the mountaineer warm.

Recycling Plastic

Plastic is cheap to make, tough, and long lasting. It is so long lasting it does not rot when it is buried in landfill sites.

Some kinds of plastic cans be recycled more easily than others. Soft drink bottles are melted and made into plastic pipes, floor tiles, and even into trousers and jackets.

Poisonous plastics and liquids such as paints and oils are collected to make them safe before recycling them.

REUSE

Lots of people throw away things that could be reused. Unwanted clothes, books, toys, and other things may not be recycled easily. But they could be used by someone else.

Garage and yard sales, rummage sales, and school fairs raise money by selling things that can be reused. Many charity shops raise money to help people or animals by selling second-hand things for reuse.

Collecting for Charity

Sort out old books and toys that other people could use. Take them to a charity shop that will pass them on to children who need them. Some charities also collect and sell used postage stamps and aluminum foil to raise money.

Household antiques on display for sale and reuse. People often pay high prices for old items.

European chimney pots removed from old houses before they were pulled down are stored for reuse.

CREATING LESS WASTE

We can all cut down on the amount of waste we produce and save energy and materials. Collect and separate newspapers, bottles, cans, and plastics that can be recycled.

Most of our garbage comes from packaging, so buy goods that use little or no packaging. Reuse empty containers for other things and pass on old clothes and toys for other people to use.

In a market in China, used cardboard boxes are collected for recycling.

A fruit vendor in Cairo, Egypt. In markets, items are usually sold "loose" and wrapped only in paper bags. This creates less waste packaging.

GLOSSARY

Aluminum A light, silvery metal that is dug out of the ground as bauxite.

Cellophane Thin but strong "see-through" paper.

Incinerator A furnace or fire for burning garbage.

Landfill site A huge hole in the ground into which crushed garbage is dumped. When the hole is filled, the site is covered with grass or used for new buildings.

Magnet A piece of iron that has been magnetized so that it can attract steel and other pieces of iron.

Material Stuff that something is made of—wood, plastic, paper, and glass are all materials.

Oil A black liquid that takes millions of years to form underground. Plastic is made from oil, and oil is burned in power plants to make electricity.

Packaging Container or wrapping that something is sold in.

Pollution Dirty or harmful waste that damages the air, water, or land.

Recycling center The place where articles such as old newspapers, bottles, cans, and plastic bottles are collected and separated, ready to be recycled.

Recycled/recycling When an object is recycled, the material it is made of is reprocessed to make something else.

Reused Used again.

Thrift shop A shop that collects and sells secondhand things and gives the money to an organization that helps people in need.

FURTHER READING

Chapman, Gillian. *Art from Rocks and Shells: With Projects Using Pebbles, Feathers, Flotsam, and Jetsam* (Salvaged). Austin, TX: Raintree Steck-Vaughn, 1995.

Kallan, Stuart A. *Eco-Games* (Target Earth). Edina, MN: Abdo and Daughters, 1993.

Parker, Steve. *Waste, Recycling and Re-Use* (Protecting Our Planet). Austin, TX: Raintree Steck-Vaughn, 1998.

Pfiffner, George. *Earth-Friendly Outdoor Fun: How to Make Fabulous Games, Gardens, and Other Projects from Reusable Objects* (Earth-Friendly). New York: John Wiley and Sons, 1996.

Savage, Candace. *Trash Attack: Garbage, and What We Can Do About It.* Buffalo, NY: Firefly Books, 1991.

Schwartz, Linda and Beverly Armstrong. *Likeable Recyclables.* Santa Barbara, CA: Learning Works, 1992.

Umnik, Sharon Dunn (ed.). *175 Easy-To-Do Everyday Crafts.* Honesdale, PA: Boyds Mills Press, 1995.

INDEX

aluminum 6, 13, 14, 19, 23, 26, 31

bags and boxes 4, 6, 8, 9, 18, 20, 28, 29
bins, recycling 18, 22
bottles 4, 6, 13, 18, 22, 25, 28

cans 4, 5, 6, 13, 14, 19, 22, 23, 28
cans, garbage 5, 6
car oil 13, 25, 31
cardboard 4, 6, 8, 19, 28
cellophane 6, 9, 31
clothes 5, 13, 26, 28
compost 15
computers 14

dustbins 5, 6, 11

Earth's resources 14
energy, saving 17, 28

garbage and refuse 4, 5, 6, 10, 13, 19, 28
glass 4, 5, 6, 9, 13, 18, 19, 22

household garbage and waste 5, 10, 13, 19

incinerators 10, 11, 14, 31

kitchen waste 5, 15

landfill sites 10, 14, 23, 31

metals 12, 13, 14, 17, 18, 20, 23

newspapers 13, 28

packaging 6, 7, 8, 9, 20, 28, 29, 31

paper 4, 5, 6, 9, 13, 14, 16, 18, 19, 20, 21, 29
plastics 4, 5, 6, 9, 13, 14, 24, 25, 28
pollution 10, 14, 31

recycling 13, 14, 17, 18, 19, 20, 21, 23, 24, 25, 26, 28, 31
recycling centers 19, 20, 31
reusing 22, 26, 27, 28, 31

scrap 5, 12, 23
secondhand items 26
sorting and separating waste 12, 13, 18, 22
steel 13, 17, 19, 23

wood pulp 16, 20

© Copyright 1998 Wayland (Publishers) Ltd.

DATE DUE

NOV 0 2 2008		
NOV 0 2 2001		
APR 1 2 2004		
JUN 0 3 2004		

GAYLORD   #3523PI   Printed in USA